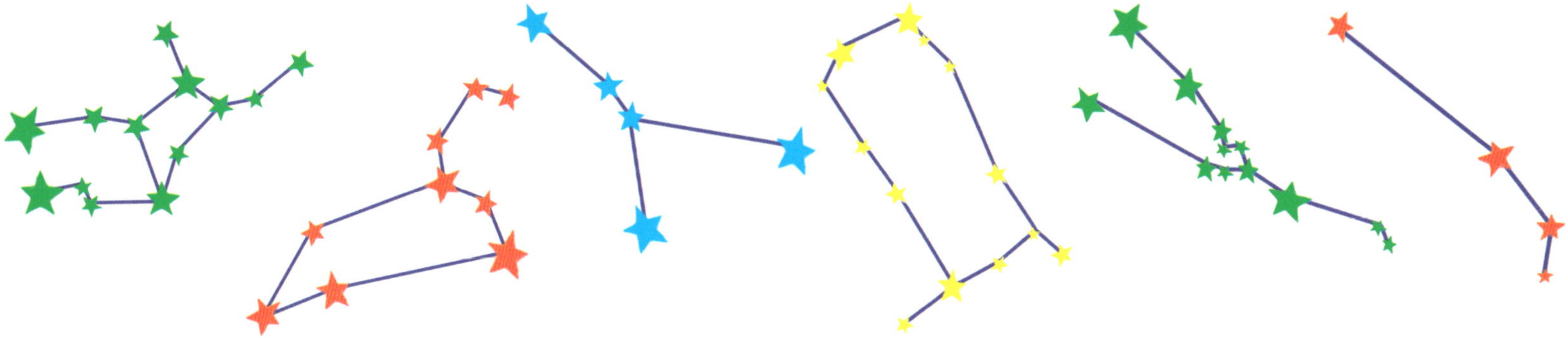

AstrologiK

KABBALISTIC ASTROLOGY GUIDE FOR CHILDREN

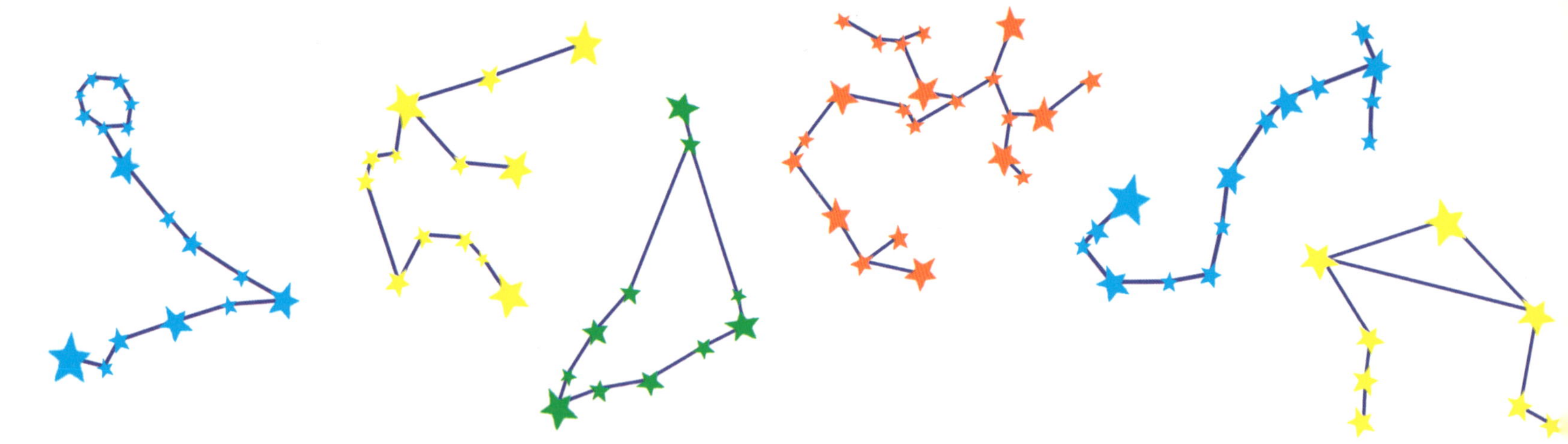

ACKNOWLEDGMENTS

To my children: Davidi (Leo), Moshe (Taurus – Aries), Chana (Gemini), Yacov (Scorpio) and Esther (Pisces).

With your various gifts and challenges you teach me the importance of really listening, truly accepting and loving unconditionally. I love you to no end, and I hope I'll be able to stay just a little out of your way so you can have the space to become the people you are meant to be.

To Rav and Karen Berg: Every small piece of wisdom and tool in this book I credit entirely to you both. The world would not have access to the wisdom of Kabbalah if not for your tireless work, selfless courage and endless dedication. I wish to be part of your mission for the rest of my life.

To my husband Yehuda: Thank you for always supporting me and for making our lives a true journey of transformation.

To Edmée: For holding my hand on this creative journey. You are a true friend and a great mentor. Thank you for helping me make this book a reality.

To Francisco: You put so much effort and detail into these magnificent illustrations; they are what make this book come alive.

Kabbalah Publishing is a registered DBA of Kabbalah Centre International, Inc.

For further information:

The Kabbalah Centre
155 E. 48th St., New York, NY 10017
1062 S. Robertson Blvd., Los Angeles, CA 90035

1.800. Kabbalah
www.kabbalah.com

First Edition, 2014
Printed in Canada
ISBN: 978-1-57189-936-1

Design: Francisco De Anda

KABBALISTIC ASTROLOGY GUIDE FOR CHILDREN

by
MICHAL BERG

Illustrated by
FRANCISCO DE ANDA

TABLE OF CONTENTS

HOW TO USE THIS BOOK

It's not by chance that you were born at a certain date in time, in a certain month and year.
Your soul chose the exact moment when the stars and the planets align in a perfect order for you to have all the tools you need to achieve what you came to do here on Earth.

In this book you will discover how Astrology, together with kabbalistic tools, can help you use your gifts and overcome your challenges. This way you can become the best you can be!

Astrology is the study of the planets and stars, and the ways they influence us. Kabbalah is an ancient wisdom that explains how the universe works and how we can receive the most out of life. To use this book, first you need to know what astrological sign you were born under; ask your parents to help you figure it out. When you go to the pages about your sign, you will find some questions that relate to your personality. With honesty and an open heart, try to see if these traits are true for you. Next, read and use all the tools that follow to get all the support you need for your spiritual growth. Finally, connect to your full potential in the last step—the affirmation.

After reading about your own sign, you can have fun reading about the astrological signs of your friends and family members in order to understand them better, and learn how to be a real friend.

You may also find that you identify with some of the characteristics that appear in other signs. This is because all the planets actually affect each and everyone of us in some way.

You can find out more about these planetary influences by having your own comprehensive astrological chart read by a professional Kabbalistic Astrologer.

(Note: There are two universal calendars – one that follows the moon [Lunar Calendar] and one that follows the sun [Gregorian Calendar]. Depending on your date of birth, and which calendar you look at, your sign might change and you could be under the influence of two signs.)

My Tool Box:

The tools presented in each sign can help you activate the energy that already exists inside of you to help you express your strengths and transform your weaknesses.

My Two Letters of the Month

Every month has two Aramaic letters: One for the ruling planet and one for the sign. You can meditate on these two letters to connect to the unique energy of your own birth month, as well as the energy of the current month of the year.

My 72 Names of God

There are 72 Names of God, which are channels for the Light Force of God. To draw extra energy and strength, meditate on the Name that corresponds to your sign.

Scanning direction right to left, top to bottom

כ·ה·ת	א·כ·א	ל·ל·ה	מ·ה·ש	ע·ל·ם	ס·י·ט	י·ל·י	ו·ה·ו
ה·ק·ם	ה·ר·י	מ·ב·ה	י·ז·ל	ה·ה·ע	ל·א·ו	א·ל·ד	ה·ז·י
ח·ה·ו	מ·ל·ה	י·י·י	נ·ל·ך	פ·ה·ל	ל·ו·ו	כ·ל·י	ל·א·ו
ו·ש·ר	ל·כ·ב	א·ו·ם	ר·י·י	ש·א·ה	י·ר·ת	ה·א·א	נ·ת·ה
י·י·ז	ר·ה·ע	ח·ע·ם	א·נ·י	מ·נ·ד	כ·ו·ק	ל·ה·ח	י·ח·ו
מ·י·ה	ע·ש·ל	ע·ר·י	ס·א·ל	י·ל·ה	ו·ו·ל	מ·י·כ	ה·ה·ה
פ·ו·י	מ·ב·ה	נ·י·ת	נ·נ·א	ע·מ·ם	ה·ח·ש	ד·נ·י	ו·ה·ו
מ·ח·י	ע·נ·ו	י·ה·ה	ו·מ·ב	מ·צ·ר	ה·ר·ח	י·י·ל	נ·מ·ם
מ·ו·ם	ה·י·י	י·ב·מ	ר·א·ה	ח·ב·ו	א·י·ע	מ·נ·ק	ד·מ·ב

My Angel

Angels are messengers of the Light that can help us when we feel sad or scared, or just need support! We do not pronounce the angel's name out loud but rather scan, and meditate on, the letters of the name.

My Body

Every astrological sign is associated with a part of the body, and we can learn about our physical and spiritual strengths and weakness by learning about that part.

My Commitment

When we make a commitment it pushes us to focus and reach our goals. Use the commitment to help you realize your dreams.

My Affirmation

To get anywhere, we need to know where we're going. The affirmation will help you see yourself as already being the best you can be.

The Illustrations

If you pay close attention to the illustrations of each sign, you will find the characters going through a process of transformation. My wish for you is that this will help you to visualize your own process of growth.

Enjoy the journey!

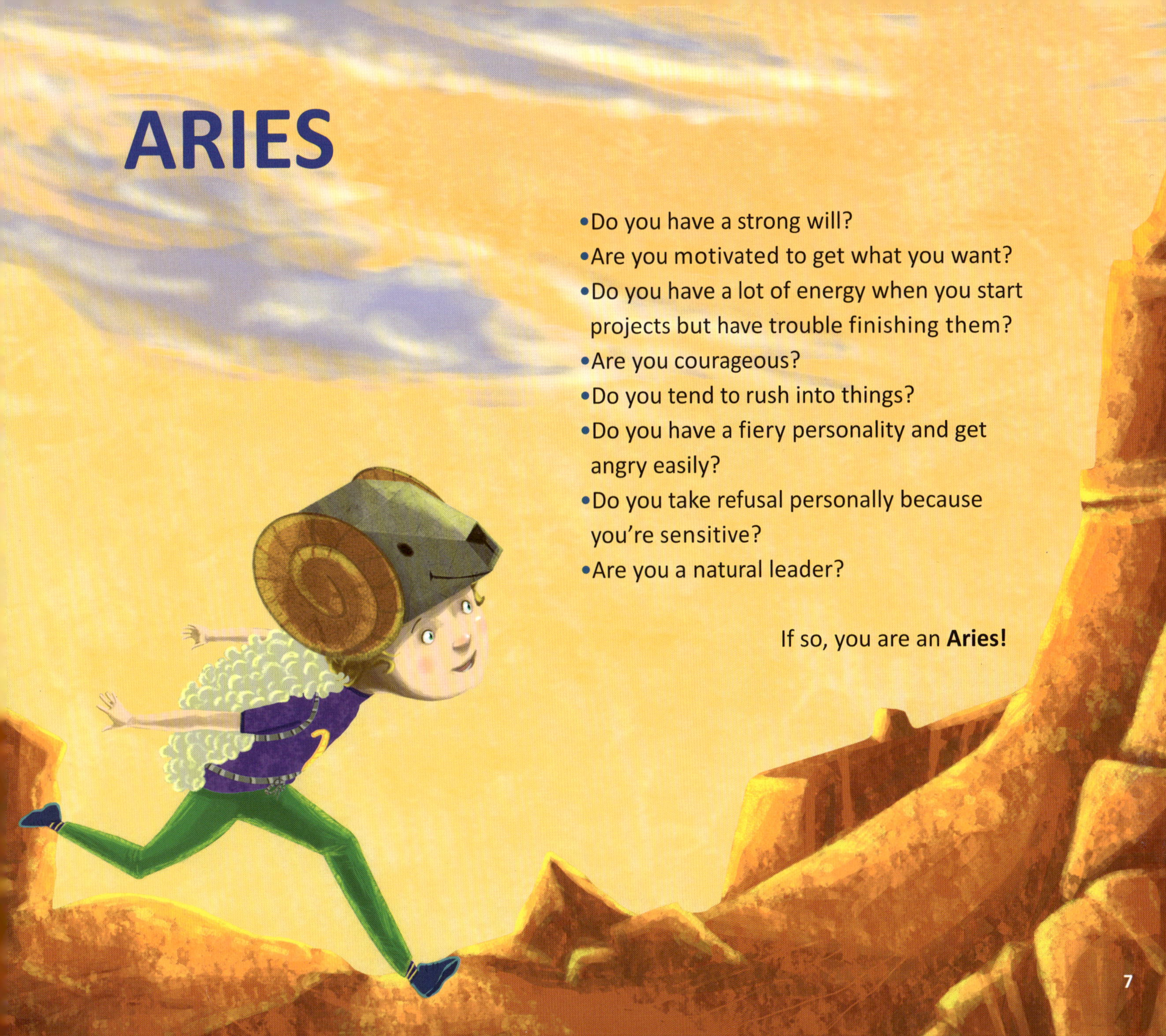

ARIES

- Do you have a strong will?
- Are you motivated to get what you want?
- Do you have a lot of energy when you start projects but have trouble finishing them?
- Are you courageous?
- Do you tend to rush into things?
- Do you have a fiery personality and get angry easily?
- Do you take refusal personally because you're sensitive?
- Are you a natural leader?

If so, you are an **Aries!**

MY LETTERS OF THE MONTH

The two Aramaic letters that are connected to my sign are ***Dalet*** for the plant Mars, and ***Hei*** for the sign of Aries. These two letters combined can help me transform my strong Desire to Receive for Myself Alone, to the Desire to Receive in Order to Share with others.

MY 72 NAMES

(Finish what you start)

I can meditate on this three-letter combination to help focus on finishing a project I have started or to achieve a goal I have set for myself.

MY ANGEL

Aries is ruled by the Angel Uriel. I can meditate on the name Uriel to help me become aware of the needs of others and open my heart so I can help them.

MY BODY

The part of the body connected to my sign is the head. This is to remind me to stop and think before I act, and not rush head first into conversations or situations.

MY COMMITMENT

I will use all these tools so I can direct my energy toward sharing and helping others.

MY AFFIRMATION

When my anger is controlled,
and I listen to others and the Light,
doors open by themselves,
with no need for me to fight.
Finishing everything I start,
means success, I am aware.
I become a real leader,
and lead my friends with love
and care.

TAURUS

- Do you like structure and routine?
- Do you take your time doing things?
- Does the idea of change frighten you?
- Do you think of safety before trying something new and different?
- Do people ever tell you that you are stubborn?
- Do you like to be in plush, comfortable surroundings?
- Do you appreciate having nice things?
- Are you loyal to your friends?

If so, you are a **Taurus!**

MY LETTERS OF THE MONTH

The two Aramaic letters that are connected to my sign are ***Pei*** for the planet Venus, and ***Vav*** for the sign of Taurus. These two letters combined can help me see the Light everywhere and in everything, and also figure out what I need to change and work on.

MY 72 NAMES

ד·נ·י

(Enough is never enough)

I meditate on this three-letter combination to awaken my desire to have and do more, and not to just settle for what I've already accomplished.

MY ANGEL

Taurus is ruled by the Angel Lahati'el. I can meditate on the name Lahati'el to help me to get out of my comfort zone so I can feel free to try new things.

MY BODY

The parts of the body that correspond to the sign of Taurus are the neck and throat. The neck is flexible and helps the head to move, showing me that I can move forward in life by being flexible and open to change.

MY COMMITMENT

I will use these tools so I can make a tiny change every day. This will eventually help me feel more at ease with bigger changes.

MY AFFIRMATION

I let go of my old habits and decide they do not matter,
I open up my eyes, to see what I can do better.
I love to have nice things, but I really only want them
because I think of others, and I want to share them!
I move forward in new ways that I never explored,
and help others connect to the Light in the world.

GEMINI

- Do you like exploring and learning about new things?
- Do you get bored easily?
- Do you often do several things at the same time?
- Do you ever feel like two different people?
- Are you able to put yourself in someone else's shoes, and start feeling and thinking like them?
- Do you like to talk and communicate?
- Do you get frustrated when people don't immediately get what you mean?
- Are you quick to judge, quick to react, and quick to change?

If so, you are a **Gemini!**

MY LETTERS OF THE MONTH

The two Aramaic letters that are connected with my sign are ***Resh*** for the planet Mercury, and ***Zayin*** for the sign of Gemini. These two letters combined can help me identify and unite my two different personalities so I can become one strong force of Light.

MY 72 NAMES

(Certainty)

I meditate on this three-letter combination to help follow the voice of the Light inside of me and trust that this will bring out the best in me, and in every situation.

MY ANGEL

The Angel Pni'el rules Gemini. I can meditate on the name Pni'el to help me to focus on my goals and to finish what I start.

MY BODY

The part of the body that corresponds to my sign is the lungs. As a Gemini, I need to learn that taking one deep breath at a time is better than taking many small ones that can tire me out. I have to remember to stop, breathe, look around, and just enjoy life.

MY COMMITMENT

I will use these tools so I can learn to be happy in the present and feel fulfilled from within.

MY AFFIRMATION

I focus and listen to my true voice,
being present is my real choice.
I do one thing at a time and all the way,
so I don´t get bored, and can be my best every day.
I have great ideas and I make them real,
making things happen is the deal!
True commitment is the key to becoming a beacon of
Light and the leader I can be.

CANCER

- Do you have a great sense of humor?
- Does your mood change often?
- Do you like lots of hugs and love all the time?
- When people criticize you, do you get upset easily?
- When you think about the future, do you ever feel scared?
- Are you sort of shy in public?
- Do you enjoy hanging out at home with your family?
- Do you care for your friends as if they are your own brothers and sisters?

If so, you are a **Cancer!**

MY LETTERS OF THE MONTH

The two Aramaic letters that are connected to my sign are ***Tav*** for the Moon, and ***Chet*** for Cancer. These two letters combined can help me overcome the mood swings that are caused by my sign being ruled by the moon.

MY 72 NAMES

(Letting go)

I meditate on this three-letter combination to help let go of my fears, and move forward with certainty and happiness.

MY ANGEL

The Angel Zuri'el rules the sign of Cancer. I can meditate on the name Zuri'el to help free me from being over-sensitive, and to develop more compassion for others.

MY BODY

The part of the body that corresponds to my sign is the stomach. My stomach is the most vulnerable part of my body; I try not to overload my belly with food, or my mind with fears and worries. Being jolly and trusting the Light helps me feel good.

MY COMMITMENT

I will use all these tools so I can control my emotions and be happy. I will try to shift my attention away from myself, to how my friends and family feel, and that way I can stay soft and loving.

MY AFFIRMATION

Feelings are the best gift that can be,
only if I'm in control, and they don't control me.
I feel for others, and I truly do care,
not to be a hero, but just to share.
The past is gone; I look forward without fear,
and I'm working on being happy each day of the year.

LEO

- Are you outgoing and friendly?
- Do you think the world is your stage?
- Is it difficult for you to ask for help?
- Do you tend to feel like you don’t have control when things happen to you?
- Do you often think that people are not fair with you?
- Is it hard for you to admit something was your fault?
- Do others look up to you as a leader?
- Do you use your charm to achieve your goals?

If so, you are a **Leo!**

MY LETTERS OF THE MONTH

כט

The two Aramaic letters that are connected to my sign are ***Caf*** for the sun, and ***Tet*** for the sign of Leo. These two letters combined can help me open up my big heart and use it to help others.

MY 72 NAMES

(Global Transformation)

I meditate on this three-letter combination to have the courage to take responsibility and become the leader I am meant to be, so I can make a difference in the world.

MY ANGEL

ברקיאל

The Angel Barki'el rules the sign of Leo. I can meditate on the name Barki'el to help me not be afraid of making mistakes and be open to learn from others.

MY BODY

The part of the body that corresponds with Leo is the heart. The heart is the most vital organ of the body and the one that works the hardest. It teaches me that being respected by others is a result of hard work and taking responsibility.

MY COMMITMENT

I will use these tools so I can control my ego, and start doing things for others even when no one sees.

MY AFFIRMATION

I take full responsibility in my life from the start,
I learn to do everything with my big loving heart.
If I don't look for the golden star,
I'll be a channel of the Light, and get really far.
To be a real king or queen I need to know how to serve,
that's how I can get the real love I deserve.

VIRGO

- Do you have a good eye for details?
- Are you picky about your food and clothes?
- Do you like things to be clean and in order?
- Do you like telling other people what to do?
- Are you critical of yourself and others?
- Do you always work on yourself to become better at everything you do?
- Do you make decisions mainly with your five senses?
- Are you a hard worker?

If so, you are a **Virgo!**

MY LETTERS OF THE MONTH

The two Aramaic letters that are connected to my sign are ***Yud*** for the sign of Virgo, and ***Resh*** for the planet Mercury. These two letters combined can help me know the spiritual order that exists in the world beyond my limited five senses.

MY 72 NAMES

(Sweetening judgment)

I meditate on this three-letter combination to help replace judgment toward others and myself with unconditional love.

MY ANGEL

The Angel Chani'el rules the sign of Virgo. I can meditate on the name Chani'el to help me let go of my fears and insecurities and trust the Light.

MY BODY

The parts of the body that correspond to Virgo are the digestive system and the intestines; this is why I might sometimes have a sensitive stomach. This helps remind me not to be so harsh with others and myself, and that when I love more I will be at peace with who I am.

MY COMMITMENT

I will use these tools so I can pause and remember that I don't see the whole picture, and to allow more time before judging a person or a situation.

MY AFFIRMATION

I look at the world from up above,
the Light's work is perfect, it fits like a glove.
I'm joyful, I'm happy, with laughter I flow,
mistakes are allowed, they do help me grow.
When I give second chances, I can be
compassionate and loving, and know it'll come back to me.

LIBRA

- Do you appreciate beauty in people, nature, and the arts?
- Do you want to make peace when you see people fighting?
- Do you usually see how both sides are right?
- Is it difficult for you to speak-up, make decisions or take a side?
- Do you want to bring harmony around the world?
- Do you have trouble starting things?
- Do you need people to like you to feel good about yourself?
- Do you prefer having company to spending time alone?

If so, you are a **Libra!**

MY LETTERS OF THE MONTH

The two Aramaic letters that are connected to my sign are ***Pei*** for the planet Venus, and ***Lamed*** for Libra. These two letters combined can help me connect to the energy of balance and harmony.

MY 72 NAMES

(Casting yourself in a favorable light)

I meditate on this three-letter combination to search and find my truth, and have the courage to stick to it.

MY ANGEL

צוריאל

The Angel Tzuri'el rules the sign of Libra. I can meditate on the name Tzuri'el to help me let go of the fear of not being liked, and connect to my inner strength and power.

MY BODY

The parts of the body that corresponds to Libra are the kidneys. Even though there are two kidneys they act like one organ and not like two. With this awareness I can develop the ability to see both sides of a story, and still be able to make decisions and have one strong voice.

MY COMMITMENT

I will use these tools to discover my own voice and desires, so I can make decisions in everyday life.

MY AFFIRMATION

When I listen to my inner voice,
I'll always make the perfect choice.
The Light shows me and helps me decide,
I'm not afraid to confront, or to take a side.
I'm not worried about being liked; I'm doing my job
to bring peace and harmony all over the globe.

SCORPIO

- Do you have the will and passion to accomplish your goals?
- Are you highly intuitive?
- Are your feelings intense?
- Do you tend to keep information a secret?
- Is it difficult for you to forgive when someone hurts you?
- When people don't give you what you want, do you think it means they don't love you?
- Do you like to be in control?
- Are you independent?

If so, you are a **Scorpio!**

MY LETTERS OF THE MONTH

דנ

The two Aramaic letters that are connected to my sign are ***Dalet*** for the planet Mars, and ***Nun*** for the sign of Scorpio. These two letters combined can help me connect to the energy of mercy so I can overcome challenges, and remember that each time I fall it's an opportunity to rise and go to a higher level.

MY 72 NAMES

ל·ה·ח

(Revealing the dark side)

I can meditate on this three-letter combination to find where negativity is hiding in me so I can remove it and let all the Light inside me shine out.

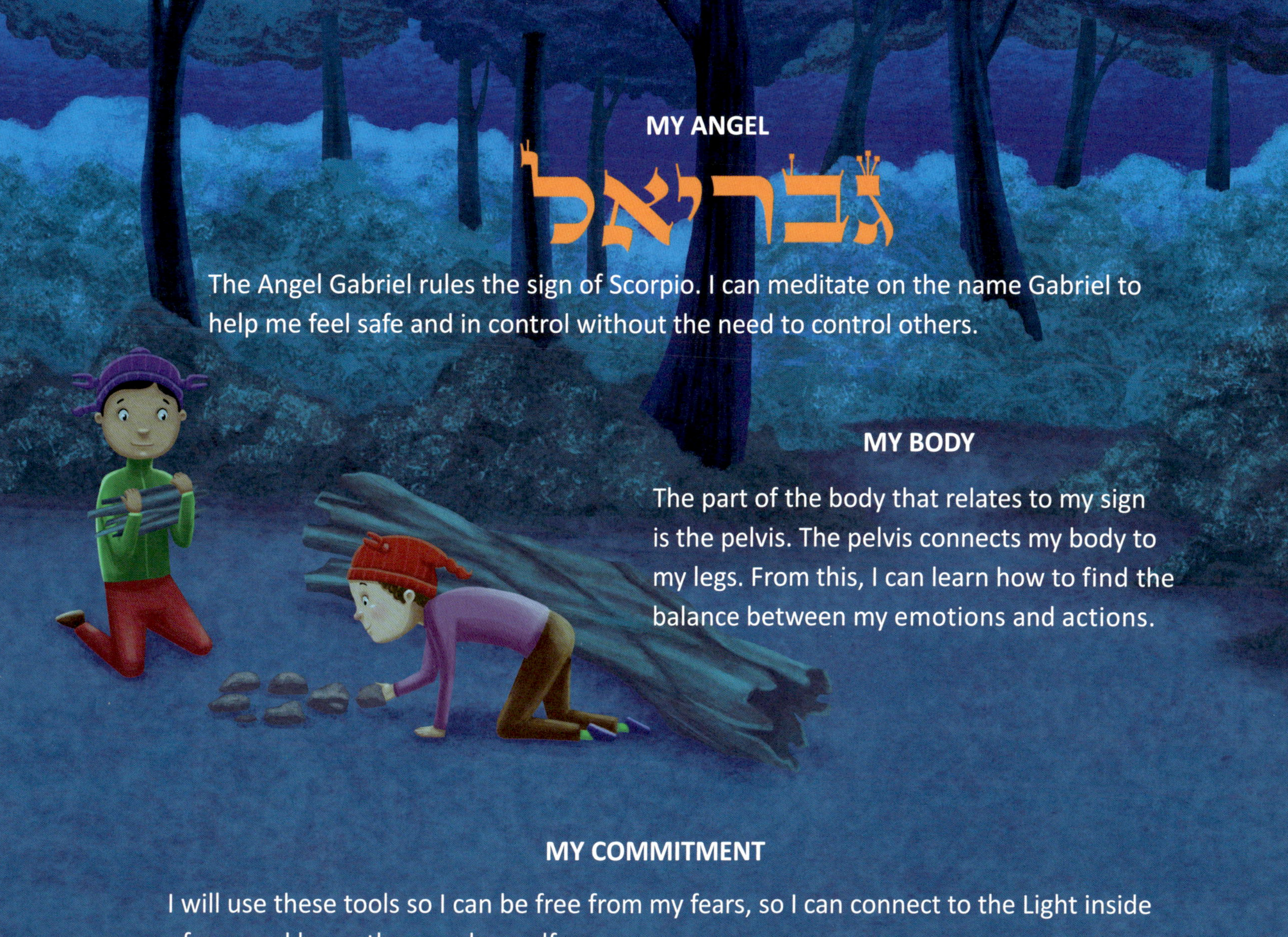

MY ANGEL

גבריאל

The Angel Gabriel rules the sign of Scorpio. I can meditate on the name Gabriel to help me feel safe and in control without the need to control others.

MY BODY

The part of the body that relates to my sign is the pelvis. The pelvis connects my body to my legs. From this, I can learn how to find the balance between my emotions and actions.

MY COMMITMENT

I will use these tools so I can be free from my fears, so I can connect to the Light inside of me, and love others and myself.

MY AFFIRMATION

I trust people, I trust the Light,
I learn to forgive, for me it's what's right.
I express my love, everyone gets a part,
especially the people who are close to my heart.
I let go of my fear, and trust that the Light
will always give me what I need, so I can lift
everyone up, and connect to the Light.

SAGITTARIUS

- Do you seek adventure and new places?
- Do you like information and sharing knowledge?
- Do you openly admit your mistakes?
- Are you quick to say what's on your mind without thinking it through?
- When you get angry, is it hard for you to snap out of it?
- Do you tend to exaggerate when you speak about things that happened?
- Do you enjoy being independent?
- Are you usually upbeat and happy?

If so, you are a **Sagittarius!**

MY LETTERS OF THE MONTH

סג

The two Aramaic letters that are connected to my sign are ***Samech*** for the sign of Sagittarius, and ***Gimel*** for the planet Jupiter. These two letters combined can help me connect to the energy of miracles, and the consciousness that everything is possible.

MY 72 NAMES

ל.ל.ן

(Speaking the right words)

I can meditate on this three-letter combination to help me choose and say the right words to others with honesty and sensitivity.

MY ANGEL

The Angel Me’adoni’el rules the sign of Sagittarius. I can meditate on the name Me’adoni’el to help me find balance between thinking that I’m not good enough, and taking responsibility for my mistakes.

MY BODY

The parts of the body that are connected to my sign are the thighs and hips. That’s why I love to move, go places, and be free. But I also need to learn how to sit still, and focus on my work.

MY COMMITMENT

I will use these tools so I can be excited and motivated without taking unnecessary risks.

MY AFFIRMATION

Before I speak I need to think,
caring is the secret, and the trick!
I act on my desire to take risks, and use my knowledge
to take on a bounty of spiritual challenges.
I learn to communicate and realize the power of words,
so I can be a channel and reveal Light in the world.

CAPRICORN

- Are you good with numbers and science?
- Do you take your time with new tasks to make sure you're doing them right?
- Do you put your responsibilities before having fun?
- Do you work well by yourself?
- Are you slow to warm up to others and smile?
- Is it difficult for you to talk about your emotions?
- Do you enjoy giving gifts as a way of expressing your love?
- Do you fight for justice?

If so, you are a **Capricorn!**

MY LETTERS OF THE MONTH

עב

The two Aramaic letters that are connected to my sign are ***Ayin*** for the sign of Capricorn, and ***Bet*** for the planet Saturn. These two letters combined equal 72 in numerology and I can use them to connect to the 72 Names of God. These Names are channels that bring the Light down to this world, so I can clearly see the connection between the physical and spiritual worlds.

MY 72 NAMES

ע·מ·ם

(Passion)

I can meditate on this three-letter combination to be passionate about life and find joy in everything I do.

MY ANGEL

The Angel Shni'el rules Capricorn. I can meditate on the name Shni'el to help me feel safe and happy, without having lots of material possessions.

MY BODY

The parts of the body that are connected to my sign are the bones and skin. The bones are like my personality—strong with a need for structure and boundaries, and the skin teaches me to also be flexible.

MY COMMITMENT

I will use these tools so I can let the Light into every part of my life.

MY AFFIRMATION

I realize the Light is my best partner,
it will make things happen without working harder.
When I learn to have fun while still being responsible,
I know that I can do the impossible.
I welcome to my life pure love and laughter,
I open my heart to others so I can live happily ever after.

AQUARIUS

- Do you have innovative ideas?
- Do you see the big picture and dislike to handle the details?
- Do you like to be unique and somewhat a rebel?
- Do people tell you that you are stubborn?
- Is it easy for you to forgive and move on?
- Do you ever forget about the people closest to you while you're focused on saving humanity?
- Do you feel that life should be fair?
- Do you want to change the world?

If so, you are an **Aquarius!**

MY LETTERS OF THE MONTH

The two Aramaic letters that are connected to my sign are ***Tzadik*** for the sign of Aquarius, and ***Bet*** for the planet Saturn. These two letters combined can help me make big things happen, change what doesn't work, and achieve real freedom—life without chaos!

MY 72 NAMES

(Seeing the big picture)

I can meditate on this three-letter combination to see how life is one big puzzle. In order to make things happen, I patiently need to take one step at a time.

MY ANGEL

Aquarius is ruled by the Angel Gabriel. I can meditate on the name Gabriel to help me be aware of the people that are close to me, listen to what they need, and be there for them.

MY BODY

The part of the body connected to my sign is the ankles. This is to teach me that I need to have structure in order to reach my goals.

MY COMMITMENT

I will use these tools so I can achieve my full potential and make a difference in the world.

MY AFFIRMATION

Being patient and persistent is my deal,
so I can make my big ideas real.
I learn to ask for help, and consider others' point of view,
this helps me see things better, and learn something new.
I have a few good friends that I truly care about,
this is how I make a difference that will surely stand out.

PISCES

- Do you have a great imagination?
- Do you drift off into daydreams a lot?
- Are you very intuitive?
- Do you feel pain when your friends are in pain?
- Do you get emotional and cry easily?
- When a challenge occurs, do you wish you could just disappear until it's over?
- Do you apply your creativity, and appreciate the arts?
- Are you the peacemaker who brings people together?

If so, you are a **Pisces!**

MY LETTERS OF THE MONTH

The two Aramaic letters that are connected to my sign are *Kuf* for the sign of Pisces, and *Gimel* for the planet Jupiter. These two letters combined can help me connect to the energy of joy.

MY 72 NAMES

(Thought into action)

I can meditate on this three-letter combination to help manifest what I imagine or dream about.

MY ANGEL

רומיאל

Pisces is ruled by the Angel Rumi'el. I can meditate on the name Rumi'el to help me use my power to overcome my oversensitive nature and deal with my challenges.

MY BODY

The part of the body that's connected to my sign is the feet. They help me to be more grounded and move things forward.

MY COMMITMENT

I will use these tools to be able to use my intuition and compassion to bring people together and help them.

MY AFFIRMATION

I use my intuition to know what's right,
I dream a lot but keep it mostly for the night.
I learn the difference between illusion and real action,
my emotions try to put me down but I control my reaction.
I move forward with strength and clarity,
using all my gifts to bring the world a knowledge of unity.

Ana Beko'ach

The Ana Beko'ach prayer is another very powerful tool for you to use! Each verse corresponds to one or more of the astrological signs and months, and using it can help you to draw the Light you need. Try to say it at least once a day, preferably in the morning so you can start each and every day in the best positive way.

(1) אנא בכח גדולת ימינך תתיר צרורה
TZERURAH TATIR YEMINCHA GEDULAT BEKO ' ACH ANA

(2) קבל רנת עמך שגבנו טהרנו נורא
NORA TAHARENU SAGVENU AMCHA RINAT KABEL

(3) נא גבור דורשי יחודך כבבת שמרם
SHAMREM KEVAVAT YICHUDCHA DORSHEI GIBOR NA

(4) ברכם טהרם רחמי צדקתך תמיד גמלם
GAMLEM TAMID TZIDKATCHA RACHAMEI TAHAREM BRACHEM

(5) חסין קדוש ברוב טובך נהל עדתך
ADATECHA NAHEL TUVCHA BEROV KADOSH CHASIN

(6) יחיד גאה לעמך פנה זוכרי קדושתך
KEDUSHATECHA ZOCHREI P ' NEH LE ' AMCHA GE ' EH YACHID

(7) שועתנו קבל ושמע צעקתנו יודע תעלומות
TA ' ALUMOT YODE ' A TZAK ' ATEINU U ' SHMA KABEL SHAV ' ATEINU

ברוך שם כבוד מלכותו לעולם ועד (SILENTLY)
VA ' ED L ' OLAM MALCHUTO KEVOD SHEM BARUCH

(1) **Capricorn and Aquarius** (2) **Sagittarius and Pisces** (3) **Aries and Scorpio** (4) **Leo**

(5) **Taurus and Libra** (6) **Gemini and Virgo** (7) **Cancer**

Dedicated To:

The Rav and Karen
endless gratitude for bringing this wisdom to the masses
and inspiring me to have courage and certainty in the Light.

The Chevre and Teachers of The Kabbalah Centre
the love and care you constantly show students,
while doing your own spiritual work, motivates me to keep pushing.

My family and friends
for giving me unconditional love, patience, and support.
The lessons you teach me are priceless.

The children of the world
for always reminding me of my connection
to the 99 Percent with simplicity and truth.

May we all continue to merit the gift of this path,
and bring an end to pain very soon.

Marla

I want to dedicate this book to my son
Michael Omri
who, like the angel MICHAEL, brings blessing to my life and opens channels of Light for me.

Special thanks to
RAV and KAREN
my teacher and all the Chevre for helping me & my son in our spiritual journey.

May all the kids of the world be blessed by having the Merit to study the wisdom of Kabbalah.

At age sixteen, MICHAL BERG discovered her spiritual path at The Kabbalah Centre. She was inspired by its mission to teach the universal wisdom of Kabbalah to everyone. She internalized that inspiration and today, over twenty years later, she is president and CEO of Spirituality for Kids, an organization founded by Karen Berg. Now an online program, www.SpiritualityforKids.com teaches the rules to the game of life by offering fun new ways for parents and children to develop spiritual consciousness and dialogue.

Michal has always been driven by the belief that not only do parents assist in the spiritual development of their kids, but children also play a significant role in a parent's potential for spiritual growth. She explores this theme in a weekly blog called Spirituality for Parents (also at www.SpiritualityforKids.com) and in lectures to parents around the world. Michal's first book *Vokabbalahry: Words of Wisdom for Kids to Live By* is a multiple award-winning title. Michal Berg lives in Los Angeles with her husband Yehuda Berg and her five children.

FRANCISCO DE ANDA Born in Mexico City. Since childhood love of drawing led him to what is now his profession and passion. He graduated from the (UNAM) National School of Arts, where he studied painting, printmaking, and illustration. His work has been exhibited in galleries and forums. He has published his work in magazines and children´s books in Mexico.

If you enjoyed ***Astrologik***, you may also like

In this book, you and your child are invited to connect with 62 key words of kabbalistic wisdom. Using language distilled to its very essence, and beautifully evocative illustrations, these pages pave the way for children to not just understand the meaning of each word, but also engage with it on the level of feeling. ***VOKABBALAHRY*** brings each of its essential concepts to life in a way that encourages readers to consider how sweet our lives can be when we make the wisdom in this book our own.

VOKABBALAHRY
Words of wisdom for kids to live by
by
Michal Berg
illustrated by
Enrique Torralba